A Fair Swap

Retold by Jenny Giles
Illustrations by Isabel Lowe

Once upon a time, a man and his wife lived on a small farm. Every day, he went out to work in the fields, while she did the housework and looked after the animals.

One evening, the man came home very tired indeed, and complained to his wife. "You are so lucky, because you can stay here at home," he grumbled, "while I have to work hard in the fields. How I wish that I had such an easy life."

The woman smiled at her husband. "If you think that my life is so easy," she said, "then tomorrow we shall have a fair swap. I shall go out to the fields, and you can do the housework."

"What a good idea!" said the man.

So, early the next morning, the woman took the sickle, and went to work in the fields.

The man could not believe his luck. What a wonderful time he was going to have!

"First of all," he decided, "I will sit down and rest while I churn the cream. I will soon have the butter made."

After he had been churning for a while, he began to feel hungry. "I will cook some sausages," he said, and he went to get them.

But as soon as his back was turned, the pig ran into the house. It smelled the cream in the churn, and rushed toward it.

Crash! Down went the churn! The cream spilled all over the floor, and the pig ran about in it, snorting and snuffling.

The man heard the noise, and ran to pick up the churn. But the cream was very slippery, and he slid across the floor, banging his head against the wall.

"Oh, help!" he cried. "Look at all the cleaning up I have to do now!"

The man put the sausages on the table and chased the pig out of the kitchen. Then he began to mop the floor. But while he was cleaning, the fire went out. "I will have to get some more wood from the shed," he said.

The dog watched him leaving the house.

And when the man came out of the shed with his arms full of wood, he was just in time to see the dog coming out of the house with the string of sausages in his mouth.

"Oh, no!" cried the man. "Come back here!" He dropped the wood and chased after the dog. While he was running past the barn, he remembered that the cow was supposed to be out in the field, eating grass.

"I know what I'll do with the cow!" said the man. "I'll put her up on the roof! She can eat the grass that is growing there, and I won't have to take her all the way to the field."

Feeling very pleased with himself, he led the cow up a plank of wood, and onto the roof. As she began to eat, he leaned against the chimney to have a rest. But then, in the distance, he could see his wife coming home. It was nearly dinner time, and he had not cooked anything for her to eat!

The man scrambled down off the roof.
He picked up the wood and put it in the
fireplace.

He filled the pot with water. "I will make some soup for our dinner," he decided.

Then he remembered that the cow was up on the roof. "She might fall off and get hurt," he said. So he took some rope up onto the roof, and tied one end around the cow. He dropped the other end down the chimney.

He went back into the house, and looked over at the fireplace.

"If I tie that end of the rope to my leg," he said thoughtfully, "the cow won't be able to wander away." So he tied the rope around his ankle, and began to cut up the vegetables for the soup.

But, just as he was putting the pot on the hearth, the cow slipped off the roof.

The man was jerked halfway up the chimney, and there he stuck.

By this time, his wife was nearly home. As she came along the path, looking forward to a good meal, what did she see but the frightened cow, hanging down from the roof!

She rushed over and cut the rope with her
sickle. The cow landed on her four legs, none
the worse for her fall, and the woman ran down
to the house to see what was going on.

To her astonishment, she saw her husband lying in the fireplace, looking very foolish indeed. "The cow has nearly been killed!" cried the woman. "And just look at this mess! The pig is inside! The cream has gone, and we have no butter. The fire is out, and there is no dinner ready for me. I have been working hard all morning, while you have done nothing. Nothing at all!"

15

The woman glared at her husband, and told him, "From now on, you will go out to work in the fields every day, and I shall look after the house."

"What a good idea!" he replied.